Holiday Piggyback Songs

Compiled by
Jean Warren

Illustrated by Marion Hopping Ekberg
Chorded by Barbara Robinson

Warren Publishing House, Inc.
P.O. Box 2250, Everett, WA 98203

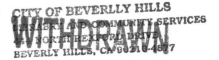

Editor: Gayle Bittinger
Contributing Editor: Elizabeth S. McKinnon
Copy Editor: Claudia G. Reid
Editorial Assistant: Deborah Bori
Typesetting: Mary Barrett, Image by Design
Layout: Kathy Jones and Cora Bunn

ISBN 0-911019-18-9

Library of Congress Catalog Number 88-050593
Printed in the United States of America
Published by: Warren Publishing House, Inc.
P.O. Box 2250
Everett, WA 98203

CONTENTS

4

May Day

Mother's Day

Father's Day

Flag Day

Fourth of July

 **Fall**

Columbus

Sung to: "Row, Row, Row Your Boat"

C
Sail, sail, sail three ships,

Slowly through the sea.

Niña, Pinta, Santa Maria,
G   C
Count them — one, two, three.

C
Land, land, land they saw,
   (Cup hand over eye.)

After many days.

Hurray, hurray for Columbus,
   (Raise arm high, as in a cheer.)
   G   C
The man who found the way!

Cathy Woolery
Tacoma, WA

Columbus Day

Sung to: "Mary Had a Little Lamb"

C
Columbus sailed the ocean blue,
G7   C
Ocean blue, ocean blue.

Columbus sailed the ocean blue,
   G7   C
In fourteen ninety-two.

C
Columbus sailed the ocean blue,
G7   C
Ocean blue, ocean blue.

I enjoy making discoveries, too.
G7   C
How about you?

Betty Loew White
Amarillo, TX

Oh, Columbus

Sung to: "Oh, My Darling Clementine"

   F
Oh, Columbus; oh, Columbus,

           C7
Sailed the ocean wide and blue.

      F
He landed in America,
C7   F
In fourteen ninety-two.

Sue Brown
Louisville, KY

Over the Ocean Blue
Sung to: "My Bonnie Lies Over the Ocean"

C   F   C
Columbus sailed over the ocean,

     D7 G
Columbus sailed over the sea.

C   F   C
Columbus discovered America,

 F   G   C
But Columbus didn't see me!

    F
Niña, Pinta,

   G   C
The Santa Maria, too.

    F
They all sailed

G   C
Over the ocean blue.

C   F   C
Columbus was looking for India,

    D7   G
But Columbus missed it, you see.

C   F   C
Columbus discovered America,

 F   G   C
But Columbus didn't see me!

    F
Niña, Pinta,

   G   C
The Santa Maria, too.

    F
They all sailed

G   C
Over the ocean blue.

Pamela Barksdale
Karen Anderson
Barrington, NH

Columbus Sailed the Ocean
Sung to: "Pop! Goes the Weasel"

D A7   D
All around the great wide world,

    A7   D
Columbus sailed the ocean

     A7   D
To prove the world was big and round.

G   A7 D
That's real devotion!

Neoma Kreuter
Ontario, CA

When You Sailed Our Way
Sung to: "Sailing, Sailing"

C   F   C
Columbus, Columbus, sailed across the sea,

 G7   C
And found a very special land

    D   G7
That belongs to you and me.

C   F   C
Columbus, Columbus, we celebrate your day,

 G7   C
In fourteen hundred and ninety-two

D   G C
When you sailed our way.

Patricia Coyne
Mansfield, MA

HALLOWEEN

Halloween Is Coming
Sung to: "I'm a Little Teapot"

C
Halloween is coming,

F   C
I like it the most.

G7   C
I'll be a goblin,

G7   C
You can be a ghost.

                              F   C
When we get all dressed up, we will say,

       F   G7   C
"Boo! It's trick or treat today!"

Becky Valenick
Mesa, AZ

Do You Know It's Halloween?
Sung to: "The Muffin Man"

    F
Oh, do you know it's Halloween,

G7   C7
Halloween, Halloween?

    F
Oh, do you know it's Halloween,

G7   C   F
This October day?

F
Ghosts and goblins are at play,

G7   C7
Are at play, are at play.

F
Ghosts and goblins are at play

G7   C   F
This October day.

Carolyn Arey
Salisbury, NC

Halloween Is Here
Sung to: "The Farmer in the Dell"

C
Halloween is here,

The munchkins now appear.

My, oh my, a witch stopped by.

        G7   C
Halloween is here.

C
Halloween is here,

Halloween is here.

An owl, a ghost, a pumpkin, too,

            G7   C
Are saying "hoot" and "boo."

C
I know they're girls and boys,

Making lots of noise.

Having fun, but soon they're done.

            G7   C
Oh, Halloween is here.

Marie Wheeler
Tacoma, WA

Halloween
Sung to: "This Old Man"

C
Halloween, Halloween,

F   G
Is a very special time,

C
With ghosts and goblins

All around,

G   C G C
Lots of candy to be found.

C
Halloween, Halloween,

F   G
Is a very special time.

C
There's a witch on her broom,

She's flying through the air.

G   C G C
I'll pretend it's me up there.

Judith Taylor Burtchet
El Dorado, KS

Halloween Song
Sung to: "Frere Jacques"

C
We are jack-o'-lanterns, we are jack-o'-lanterns,

Watch us grin, watch us grin.

We can make some silly faces,

We can make some silly faces.

C
Grin with us! Grin with us!

C
We are witches, we are witches,

Riding our brooms, riding our brooms.

We can ride all around,

In and all about the town.

C
Ride with us! Ride with us!

C
We are black bats, we are black bats,

Flapping our wings, flapping our wings.

We can fly all around,

In and all about the town.

C
Fly with us! Fly with us!

C
We are goblins, we are goblins,

We'll scare you, we'll scare you.

We can do a spooky dance,

We can do a spooky dance.

C
Dance with us! Dance with us!

Colraine Pettipaw Hunley
Doylestown, PA

I'm a Little Pumpkin
Sung to: "I'm a Little Teapot"

C
I'm a little pumpkin,

F   C
Orange and round.
   (Hold arms in circle above head.)

G7   C
When I'm sad,

G7   C
My face wears a frown.
   (Frown.)

                    F   C
But when I am happy, all aglow,

       F   G7   C
Watch my smile just grow and grow!
   (Smile.)

Barbara Hasson
Portland, OR

Here Is a Big Pumpkin
Sung to: "Mary Had a Little Lamb"

C
Here is a big pumpkin,

   G7   C
Big pumpkin, big pumpkin.

Here is a big pumpkin,

G7   C
Round and fat and orange.

C
Then you cut a funny face,

G7   C
Funny face, funny face.

Then you cut a funny face,

       G7   C
And it's a jack-o'-lantern.

Peggy Wolf
Pittsburgh, PA

I Picked a Pumpkin
Sung to: "Oh, My Darling Clementine"

   F
I picked a pumpkin, a big fat pumpkin,

                        C7
That was growing on a vine.

                    F
I carved a jack-o'-lantern,

          C7   F
And it turned out just fine.

Sue Brown
Louisville, KY

There Once Was a Pumpkin
Sung to: "I'm a Little Teapot"

C
There once was a pumpkin

F   C
Short and fat,

   G7   C
Alone in the garden

G7   C
There he sat.

                    F   C
A little girl picked him from the vine,

        F   G7   C
Took him home and said, "He's mine!"

C
She carved a funny face

      F   C
With a great big smile,

G7   C
Put in a candle

      G7   C
And after a while,

                  F   C
He wasn't a pumpkin short and fat,

      F   G7   C
He was a jack-o'-lantern — just like that!

Lynne Speaker
Olympia Fields, IL

Little Pumpkin
Sung to: "I'm a Little Teapot"

C   F   C
I'm a little pumpkin, look at me.

G7   C   G7   C
I'm as round and cute as can be.

              F   C
Carve a face, add a candle bright,

         F   G7   C
I'll glow and glow all through the night.

Deborah A. Roessel
Flemington, NJ

Pumpkin Song
Sung to: "I'm a Little Teapot"

C
I'm a little pumpkin,

F   C
Orange and round.
    (Hold arms out in a circle.)

G7   C
Here is my stem,
    (Place fist on head.)

G7   C
There is the ground.
    (Point down.)

When I get all cut up,
    ("Cut" palm with hand.)

F   C
Don't you shout!
    (Shake head and wave finger.)

            F
Just open me up
    ("Open" top of head with hand.)

    G7   C
And scoop me out!
    ("Scoop out" tummy.)

Nancy Nason Biddinger
Brian Biddinger
Orlando, FL

Did You Hear a Ghostly Sound?
Sung to: "London Bridge"

C
Did you hear a ghostly sound?

G7   C
Stand real still, look around.

Do you think a ghost is near?

G7   C
Boo! Boo! Boo!

                            Sue Brown
                     Louisville, KY

Ghost Chant

Ghost so scary,

Ghost so white,

Don't scare (child's name)

On Halloween night!

Have the children sit in a circle as they repeat the chant. Be sure to include every child's name in the chanting fun.

                       Betty Silkunas
                       Lansdale, PA

This Old Ghost
Sung to: "This Old Man"

C
This old ghost, he played one,

F   G
He played peek-a-boo on the run.

        C
With a boo! boo! boo! and a clap, clap, snap,

G   C   G C
This old ghost is a friendly chap.

C
This old ghost, he played two.

F   G
He played peek-a-boo in a shoe.

        C
With a boo! boo! boo! and a clap, clap, snap,

G   C   G C
This old ghost is a friendly chap.

C
This old ghost, he played three.

F   G
He played peek-a-boo behind a tree.

        C
With a boo! boo! boo! and a clap, clap, snap,

G   C   G C
This old ghost is a friendly chap.

                       Karen L. Brown
                     Bentonville, AR

Peek-A-Boo
Sung to: "Skip to My Lou"

F
Peek-a-boo, I see you,

C7
Peek-a-boo, I see you,

F
Peek-a-boo, I see you.

C7   F
It is Halloween time!

Colraine Pettipaw Hunley
Doylestown, PA

On Halloween Night
Sung to: "The Mulberry Bush"

D
We will go out into the night.

A7
What a sight! Such a fright!

D
We'll scare everyone in sight,

A7   D
On Halloween night!

Barbara Paxson
Warren, OH

We're Not Afraid
Sung to: "Twinkle, Twinkle, Little Star"

C   F   C
Ghosts and goblins, cats and bats,

G7   C   G7   C
We're not afraid of this or that.

G7   C   G7
They are only make-believe,

C   G7   C   G7
Funny costumes on Halloween.

C   F   C
Ghosts and goblins, cats and bats,

G7   C   G7   C
We're not afraid of this or that.

Karen L. Brown
Bentonville, AR

Being Afraid
Sung to: "Twinkle, Twinkle, Little Star"

C   F   C
Being afraid is a scary thing,

G7   C G7   C
And everyone feels the same.

G7   C   G7
Afraid of darkness, afraid of ghosts,

C   G7   C   G7
Afraid of noises and being alone.

C   F   C
Being afraid is a scary thing,

G7   C   G7   C
But it's okay to feel afraid.

Kristine Wagoner
Pacific, WA

I'm a Little Spider
Sung to: "I'm a Little Teapot"

C
I'm a little spider,

F   C
Watch me spin.

G7   C
If you'll be my dinner,

   G7   C
I'll let you come in.

                    F   C
Then I'll spin my web to hold you tight,

                F   G7   C
And gobble you up in one big bite!

Sue Brown
Louisville, KY

I Want to Be a Ghost
Sung to: "Did You Ever See a Lassie?"

       C
Oh, I want to be a ghost,

  G7   C
A ghost, a ghost.

       C
Oh, I want to be a ghost,

   G7   C
On Halloween night.

Repeat, letting the children name different things they want to be for Halloween.

Elizabeth McKinnon

Three Black Cats
Sung to: "Three Blind Mice"

C   G7   C   G7   C
Three black cats, three black cats,

   G7   C   G7   C
With big green eyes, with big green eyes.

                G7   C
They meow and cry all through the night,

                      G7   C
They jump from the fence and they run in fright,

                G7   C
They hiss at the witches, oh my, what a sight.

             G7   C
Those three black cats!

Deborah A. Roessel
Flemington, NJ

October Song
Sung to: "Frere Jacques"

C
This is October, this is October,

Halloween, Halloween.

It is so colorful,

It is so colorful.

C
Autumn time, autumn time.

Debbie Zanaty
Birmingham, AL

THANKSGIVING

Hurray, It's Thanksgiving Day!
Sung to: "When Johnny Comes Marching Home"

The Pilgrims are coming to celebrate,
^{Em}

Hurray! Hurray!
^G

The Pilgrims are coming to celebrate
^{Em}

Thanksgiving Day.
^B

The Pilgrims are coming, so don't be late,
^G ^D

We'll eat and dance to celebrate.
^{Em} ^B

And we'll all be glad, so
^{Em Am Em B}

Hurry and don't be late!
^{Em}

The Indians are coming to celebrate,
^{Em}

Hurray! Hurray!
^G

The Indians are coming to celebrate
^{Em}

Thanksgiving Day.
^B

The Indians are coming, so don't be late,
^G ^D

We'll eat and dance to celebrate.
^{Em} ^B

And we'll all be glad, so
^{Em Am Em B}

Hurry and don't be late!
^{Em}

Additional verse: "(Child's name) is coming to celebrate."

Jean Warren

Indians and Pilgrims
Sung to: "The Farmer in the Dell"

The friendly Indians came,
^C

The friendly Pilgrims came,

Heigh-ho the derry-oh,

On Thanksgiving Day.
^{G7} ^C

They came to celebrate,
^C

They came to celebrate,

Heigh-ho the derry-oh,

On Thanksgiving Day.
^{G7} ^C

June Meckel
Andover, MA

We Are Thankful
Sung to: "Frere Jacques"

C
We are thankful, we are thankful,

For our families, for our families.

On Thanksgiving Day,

You will hear us say
C
Thank you, thank you.

C
We are thankful, we are thankful,

For our friends, for our friends.

On Thanksgiving Day,

You will hear us say
C
Thank you, thank you.

C
We are thankful, we are thankful,

For our food, for our food.

On Thanksgiving Day,

You will hear us say
C
Thank you, thank you.

Repeat, letting the children name other
things for which they are thankful.

Gayle Bittinger

I Will Be a Helping Indian
Sung to: "Ten Little Indians"

C
I will be a helping Indian,

G7
I will be a helping Indian,

C
I will be a helping Indian,

G7   C
I will show you how!

C
I will help to clean the teepee,

G7
I will help to clean the teepee,

C
I will help to clean the teepee,

G7   C
I will show you how!

Have the children sing this song at cleanup
times during Thanksgiving week.

Sue Brown
Louisville, KY

Thanksgiving Day Thanks
Sung to: "The Farmer in the Dell"

C
Thanksgiving Day is here,

Thanksgiving Day is here.

Let's give thanks for all we have,
         G7   C
Thanksgiving Day is here.

C
For all our moms and dads,

For all our families,

Let's give thanks for all we have,
         G7   C
Thanksgiving Day is here.

C
For all the flowers and trees,

For all the birds and bees,

Let's give thanks for all we have,
         G7   C
Thanksgiving Day is here.

Let the children help make up new verses by telling things that they are thankful for.

**Patricia Coyne
Mansfield, MA**

I'm Thankful
Sung to: "Mary Had a Little Lamb"

C
I'm thankful for my friends at school,
G7   C
Friends at school, friends at school.

I'm thankful for my friends at school,
G7   C
And my teacher, too!

C
I'm thankful for my family,
G7   C
Family, family.

I'm thankful for my family,
G7   C
And my home, too.

Let the children take turns saying what they are thankful for and then add new verses to the song.

**Sue Brown
Louisville, KY**

It Is Thanksgiving
Sung to: "Frere Jacques"

C
It is Thanksgiving, it is Thanksgiving,

We are Indians, we are Indians.

We have come in peace,

We have come in peace.
C
Happy day, happy day.

C
It is Thanksgiving, it is Thanksgiving,

We are Pilgrims, we are Pilgrims.

This is a new beginning,

This is a new beginning.
C
Happy day, happy day.

C
It is Thanksgiving, it is Thanksgiving,

We are thankful, we are thankful,

That we can share,

That we can share.
C
Happy day, happy day.

Saundra Winnett
Lewisville, TX

On Thanksgiving Day
Sung to: "Mary Had a Little Lamb"

C
Turkey is so good to eat,
G7   C
Good to eat, good to eat.

Turkey is so good to eat,
G7   C
On Thanksgiving Day.

C
Friends and family gather round,
G7   C
Gather round, gather round.

Friends and family gather round,
G7   C
On Thanksgiving Day.

C
For all these blessings we give thanks,
G7   C
We give thanks, we give thanks.

For all these blessings we give thanks,
G7   C
On Thanksgiving Day.

Maureen Gutyan
Williams Lake, B.C.

Just Like That!

Sung to: "Frere Jacques"

C
Mr. Turkey, Mr. Turkey,

Big and fat, big and fat.

I am going to eat you,

I am going to eat you.

C
Just like that! Just like that!

Barbara Dunn
Hollidaysburg, PA

Gobble, Gobble

Sung to: "Pop! Goes the Weasel"

C   G   C
A turkey is a funny bird,

             G   C
His head goes wobble, wobble.

        G   C
He knows just one funny word —

F   G   C
Gobble, gobble, gobble.

Lynn Beaird
Loma Linda, CA

Hello, Mr. Turkey

Sung to: "If You're Happy and You Know It"

G   D
Hello, Mr. Turkey, how are you?

                          G
Hello, Mr. Turkey, how are you?

        C
With a gobble, gobble, gobble,

         G
And a wobble, wobble, wobble,

D   G
Hello, Mr. Turkey, how are you?

Barbara H. Jackson
Denton, TX

Mr. Turkey

Sung to: "Oh, My Darling Clementine"

F
Mr. Turkey, Mr. Turkey,

                      C7
Are you getting nice and fat?

                        F
We are waiting for Thanksgiving,

      C7   F
Now what do you think of that?

F
Mr. Turkey, Mr. Turkey,

                  C7
Do you ever wonder why

                        F
People eat you at Thanksgiving,

    C7   F
And not chicken pot pie?

Debra Lindahl
Libertyville, IL

Mr. Turkey, Better Watch Out!
Sung to: "Yankee Doodle"

C   G7
Mr. Turkey, better watch out,

        C   G
Thanksgiving Day is coming.

C   F
If you're not careful, you'll end up

   G7   C
In someone's hungry tummy!

F
Mr. Turkey, run, run, run,

      C
Please run away and hide.

F
Mr. Turkey, run, run, run,

      C   G7   C
Don't wait around outside!

Maureen Gutyan
Williams Lake, B.C.

Run, Little Turkey
Sung to: "Skip to My Lou"

F
Run, little turkey, run away,

C7
Run, little turkey, run away.

F
You'll be a dinner on Thanksgiving Day,

    C7   F
So run, little turkey, run away.

F
Gobble, gobble, you can't catch me,

C7
Gobble, gobble, you can't catch me.

F
I'll run away and I'll be free,

C7   F
Gobble, gobble, you can't catch me.

Sue Brown
Louisville, KY

Tom, Tom Turkey
Sung to: "Frere Jacques"

C
Tom, Tom Turkey; Tom, Tom Turkey,

Run away, run away.

Thanksgiving Day is coming,

Thanksgiving Day is coming.

C
Yum, yum, yum; run, run, run!

Bonnie Woodard
Shreveport, LA

 **Winter**

HANUKKAH

Hanukkah, Hanukkah
Sung to: "Three Blind Mice"

C G7 C   G7 C
Hanukkah, Hanukkah,

     G7   C   G7   C
Hanukkah is here, Hanukkah is here.

         G7   C
Light eight candles in a row,

         G7   C
Light eight candles and see them glow,

         G7   C
Light eight candles so we will know

            G7 C
That Hanukkah is here.

Carla C. Skjong
Tyler, MN

Sing a Song of Hanukkah
Sung to: "Did You Ever See a Lassie?"

     F
Oh, sing a song of Hanukkah,

C   F
Hanukkah, Hanukkah,

Sing a song of Hanukkah,

C   F
Happy holiday!

     C7   F
With presents and presents,

     C7   F
On every night, presents.

Oh, sing a song of Hanukkah,

    C7   F
A happy holiday!

Gillian Whitman
Westfield, NJ

Hanukkah Is Here
Sung to: "Row, Row, Row Your Boat"

C
Hanukkah is here,

Hanukkah is here.

Eight tall candles in a row,

G   C
Hanukkah is here.

C
Hanukkah is here,

Hanukkah is here.

Light the candles one by one,

G   C
Hanukkah is here.

Carla C. Skjong
Tyler, MN

Lighting All the Candles
Sung to: "I've Been Working on the Railroad"

G
I am lighting all the candles

C   G
On this Hanukkah night.

I am lighting all the candles

     A7   D7
To see them shining bright.

                              G
Flicker, flicker, little candles,

C   B7
Fill me with your glow.

C   G
Now the time has come to count them,

       D7   G
Ready, set and go —

1-2-3-4-5-6-7-8.

Gillian Whitman
Westfield, NJ

Eight Candles
Sung to: "Frere Jacques"

C
Eight candles, eight candles,

I can't wait, I can't wait.

Hanukkah is here,

We celebrate each year.

C
Hanukkah, Hanukkah.

C
Eight candles, eight candles,

I can't wait, I can't wait.

We count the lights,

Shining so bright.

C
Hanukkah, Hanukkah.

Susan Peters
Upland, CA

Light the Candles Bright
Sung to: "The Farmer in the Dell"

Oh, light the candles bright,
(F)

And dance around the light.

Heigh-ho the derry-oh,

It's Hanukkah tonight.
(C) (F)

Spin the dreidel round,
(F)

And watch it falling down.

Heigh-ho the derry-oh,

It's Hanukkah tonight.
(C) (F)

Latke treats to eat,
(F)

And family to greet.

Heigh-ho the derry-oh,

It's Hanukkah tonight.
(C) (F)

Gillian Whitman
Westfield, NJ

Hanukkah Menorah
Sung to: "A-Tisket, A-Tasket"

Menorah, menorah,
(C)

Hanukkah menorah,

Light the lights and give a gift.
(G7)

Hanukkah menorah.
(C)

Barbara Paxson
Warren, OH

Eight Little Candles
Sung to: "Twinkle, Twinkle, Little Star"

Eight little candles in a row,
(C) (F) (C)

Waiting to join the holiday glow.
(G7) (C) (G7) (C)

We will light them one by one,
(G7) (C) (G7)

Until all eight have joined the fun.
(C) (G7) (C) (G7)

Eight little candles burning bright,
(C) (F) (C)

Filling the world with holiday light.
(G7) (C) (G7) (C)

Jean Warren

Happy Hanukkah
Sung to: "I'm a Little Teapot"

Hanukkah is coming very soon,
(C) (F) (C)

I know there'll be some presents, too.
(G7) (C) (G7) (C)

Here is a menorah, light the lights,
(F) (C)

There is one for every night.
(F) (G7) (C)

1-2-3-4-5-6-7-8 — Happy Hanukkah!

Carol Harvey
Maureen Podojil
Carol DeJoy
Menton, OH

I'm a Little Dreidel
Sung to: "I'm a Little Teapot"

C
I'm a little dreidel

F　　　C
Made of clay.

G7　　　C
Spin me around

　　　G　　　　C
When you want to play.

　　　　　　　F　　　C
When I fall down, if you don't win,

F　　　　　　　G7　C
Just pick me up and spin again!

Adapted Traditional

Dreidel Song
Sung to: "I'm a Little Teapot"

C　　　　　　　　F　　C
I'm a little dreidel spinning round,

G7　　　　　　C　　G7　C
Turning, turning and falling down.

　　　　　　　　　　F　　C
Spinning faster, faster — slowing down,

　　　　F　　　G7　C
Slower, slower — fall to the ground.

Gillian Whitman
Westfield, NJ

I Am Opening a Present
Sung to: "Did You Ever See a Lassie?"

I am opening a present,
F

C7   F
A present, a present.

I am opening a present,

C7   F
It's Hanukkah tonight.

C7   F
I'll untie the ribbon,

C7   F
And take off the paper.

I am opening a present,

C7   F
It's Hanukkah tonight.

Gillian Whitman
Westfield, NJ

The Latkes Are Frying in the Pan
Sung to: "When Johnny Comes Marching Home"

Em   G
The latkes are frying in the pan, hurrah, hurrah!

Em   B
The latkes are frying in the pan, hurrah, hurrah!

G   D
And when they've cooked so nice and brown,

Em   B
We'll take them out and sit right down.

        Em Am   Em B Em
And we'll eat those yummy latkes this Hanukkah night!

Gillian Whitman
Westfield, NJ

I've Been Waiting for Christmas
Sung to: "I've Been Working on the Railroad"

G
I've been waiting for Christmas,

C   G
And it's almost here.

I've been waiting for Christmas,

A7   D7
Santa's getting near.

           G
Can't you hear the sleigh bells ringing?

C   B7
Reindeer up so high.

C   G
Can't you hear the children singing,

    D7   G
As they watch the sky?

G
Santa, hurry up,

C
Santa, hurry up,

D   G
Santa, hurry up today-ay-ay.

Santa, hurry up,

C
Santa, hurry up,

D   G
Santa, hurry up today.

G
Toys in the sleigh with Santa,

        D
Toys in the sleigh I know-oh-oh-oh.

G   C
Toys in the sleigh with Santa,

G   D G
Waiting's oh, so slow!

Elizabeth Vollrath
Stevens Pt., WI

Christmas Star
Sung to: "Twinkle, Twinkle, Little Star"

C   F   C
Twinkle, twinkle, Christmas star,

G7   C   G7   C
Way up high is where you are.

      G7   C G7
Shining there for all to see,

C   G7   C   G7
On the tiptop of our tree.

C   F   C
Twinkle, twinkle, star so bright,

G7   C   G7   C
Shine up there till morning light.

Bonnie Woodard
Shreveport, LA

Advent Song
Sung to: "Twinkle, Twinkle, Little Star"

C   F   C
Advent is a time to wait,

G7   C   G7 C
Not quite time to celebrate.

C   G7   C   G7
Light the candles one by one,

C   G7   C   G7
Till this Advent time is done.

C
Christmas Day will soon be here,

G7   C   G7   C
Time for joy and time for cheer!

Karen Leslie
Erie, PA

This Is Christmastime
Sung to: "Mary Had a Little Lamb"

C
One little Santa bouncing up and down,

G7   C
Bouncing up and down, bouncing up and down.

One little Santa bouncing up and down,

   G7   C
For this is Christmastime.

C
Two little snowflakes flying through the air,

G7   C
Flying through the air, flying through the air.

Two little snowflakes flying through the air,

   G7   C
For this is Christmastime.

C
Three little Christmas trees standing in a row,

G7   C
Standing in a row, standing in a row.

Three little Christmas trees standing in a row,

   G7   C
For this is Christmastime.

C
Four little snowmen skipping down the street,

G7   C
Skipping down the street, skipping down the street.

Four little snowmen skipping down the street,

   G7   C
For this is Christmastime.

C
Five little elves making Christmas toys,

G7   C
Making Christmas toys, making Christmas toys.

Five little elves making Christmas toys,

   G7   C
For this is Christmastime.

Vivian Sasser
Independence, MO

Christmas Day Is Coming
Sung to: "London Bridge"

C
Christmas Day is coming soon,

G7   C
Coming soon, coming soon.

Christmas Day is coming soon.

G   C
(I heard Santa say.)

C
Jingle, jingle ring the bells,

G7   C
Ring the bells, ring the bells.

Jingle, jingle ring the bells,

G   C
On old Santa's sleigh.

C
"Ho-ho-ho!" says Santa Claus,

G7   C
Santa Claus, Santa Claus.

"Ho-ho-ho!" says Santa Claus,

G   C
"I'll soon be on my way!"

C
Merry Christmas everyone,

G7   C
Everyone, everyone!

Merry Christmas everyone!

G   C
It's almost Christmas Day.

Joan Nydigger
Kent, WA

Where Is Santa?

Sung to: "Frere Jacques"

C
Where is Santa? Where is Santa?
(Put hands behind back.)

Here I am! Here I am!
(Make a big belly with arms.)

Merry, Merry Christmas!
(Sing in Santa voice.)

Merry, Merry Christmas!

C
Ho-ho-ho! Ho-ho-ho!
(Put hands behind back.)

Debbie Heller
Upper Saddle River, NJ

Hello, Santa

Sung to: "Frere Jacques"

C
Hello, Santa. Hello, Santa.

How are you? How are you?

Busy making games,

Checking children's names.

C
How are you? How are you?

C
Hello, Elves. Hello, Elves.

How are you? How are you?

Busy wrapping toys,

For the girls and boys.

C
How are you? How are you?

C
Hello, Rudolph. Hello, Rudolph.

How are you? How are you?

Landing on your toes,

Shining up your nose.

C
How are you? How are you?

Kristine Wagoner
Pacific, WA

S-A-N-T-A

Sung to: "Old MacDonald Had a Farm"

F   Bᵇ   F
Who laughs this way — "Ho-ho-ho?"

     C7 F
S-A-N-T-A!

                              Bᵇ   F
Who drives the sleigh through sleet or snow?

     C7 F
S-A-N-T-A!

His hair is white, his suit is red,

He wears a hat to cover his head.

                    Bᵇ   F
Who brings fun for girls and boys?

     C7 F
S-A-N-T-A!

Debra Lindahl
Libertyville, IL

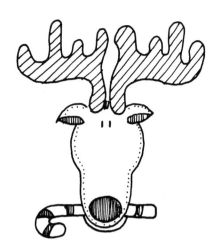

Did You Ever See a Reindeer?
Sung to: "Did You Ever See a Lassie?"

F
Did you ever see a reindeer,

C7   F
A reindeer, a reindeer?

Did you ever see a reindeer

    C7   F
With a bright shiny nose?

C7   F
A bright shiny nose,

C7   F
A bright shiny nose.

Did you ever see a reindeer

    C   F
With a bright shiny nose?

F
Oh, his name is Rudolph,

C7   F
Is Rudolph, is Rudolph.

Oh, his name is Rudolph

    C7   F
The Red-Nosed Reindeer.

    C7   F
The Red-Nosed Reindeer,

    C7   F
The Red-Nosed Reindeer.

Oh, his name is Rudolph,

    C   F
The Red-Nosed Reindeer.

Cheryl Heltne
Katy, TX

Christmastime
Sung to: "This Old Man"

C
Christmastime, Christmastime,

F   G
Is a very special time,

              C
With a tree and gifts and goodies to eat.

G   C G C
Christmastime is really neat!

Judith Taylor Burtchet
El Dorado, KS

There's a Little Elf
Sung to: "If You're Happy and You Know It"

There's a little elf that's sitting on my nose,
(G)   (D)

There's a little elf that's sitting on my nose.
(G)

He is sitting on my nose,
(C)

Then off away he goes.
(G)

Now there's no little elf on my nose.
(D)   (G)

There's a little elf that's sitting on my knee,
(G)   (D)

There's a little elf that's sitting on my knee.
(G)

He is sitting on my knee,
(C)

Just watch and he will flee.
(G)

Now there's no little elf on my knee.
(D)   (G)

There's a little elf that's sitting on my head,
(G)   (D)

There's a little elf that's sitting on my head.
(G)

He is sitting on my head,
(C)

Then away he goes to bed.
(G)

Now there's no little elf on my head.
(D)   (G)

Debbie Jones
Richland, WA

Christmastime Is Near
Sung to: "The Farmer in the Dell"

Oh, Christmastime is near,
(C)

Oh, Christmastime is near.

Santa Claus is coming soon,

Oh, Christmastime is near.
(G)   (C)

We'll decorate the tree,
(C)

We'll decorate the tree.

Put an angel on the top,

We'll decorate the tree.
(G)   (C)

Carla C. Skjong
Tyler, MN

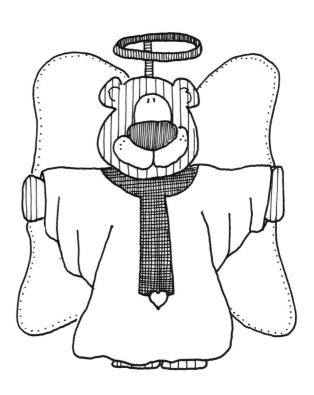

We'll Decorate the Tree
Sung to: "The Farmer in the Dell"

C
We'll decorate the tree,

We'll decorate the tree.

Heigh-ho, it's Christmastime,
      G   C
We'll decorate the tree.

C
The presents we will wrap,

The presents we will wrap.

Heigh-ho, it's Christmastime,
      G   C
The presents we will wrap.

C
Carols we will sing,

Carols we will sing.

Heigh-ho, it's Christmastime,
      G   C
Carols we will sing.

Maureen Gutyan
Williams Lake, B.C.

Twinkle, Twinkle, Little Tree
Sung to: "Music, Music, Music"

F
Twinkle, twinkle, little tree,

Twinkle, twinkle just for me.
G7   C7
All you do the whole day through

  F
Is twinkle, twinkle, twinkle.
C7   F
Christmas, a time for wishes,

         C7
A time for all the little girls and boys
  F   Cdim   Gm   C7
To fill their hearts with Christmas joys.

   F
So twinkle, twinkle, little tree,

Twinkle, twinkle just for me.
G7   C7
How I love to watch you shine

     F
And twinkle, twinkle, twinkle!

Jean Warren

Little Green Tree
Sung to: "I'm a Little Teapot"

C   F   C
I'm a little green tree in the house,
G7   C
Here is my trunk,
   (Raise arms straight up.)
G7   C
Here are my boughs.
   (Hold arms out to sides.)

               F
Decorate me now with lights so fine,
   (Move hands back and forth across body.)

          F   G7   C
Then plug them in and watch me shine!
   (Hold arms to sides and smile.)

Billie Taylor
Sioux City, IA

Christmas Bells
Sung to: "The Muffin Man"

Oh, do you hear the Christmas bells,
^F

The ^{G7}Christmas bells, the ^{C7}Christmas bells?

Oh, do you hear the Christmas bells
^F

That ^{G7}ring out ^Cloud and ^Fclear?

Oh, can you see our Christmas tree,
^F

Our ^{G7}Christmas tree, our ^{C7}Christmas tree?

Oh, can you see our Christmas tree?
^F

It ^{G7}fills the ^Croom with ^Fcheer.

Oh, do you smell the gingerbread,
^F

The ^{G7}gingerbread, the ^{C7}gingerbread?

Oh, do you smell the gingerbread?
^F

I'm ^{G7}glad Christ^{C7}mas is ^Fhere.

Maureen Gutyan
Williams Lake, B.C.

Happy Christmas Day
Sung to: "Jingle Bells"

^F
Ring the bell, ring the bell,

Christmastime is here.

^{C7}
Ring the bell, ring the ^Fbell,

^{G7}
Give a great big ^{C7}cheer!

^F
Light the lights, light the lights,

Happy Christmas Day.

^{C7}
Light the lights, light the ^Flights,

^{C7}
Shout a big "Hur^Fray!"

Carla C. Skjong
Tyler, MN

Hear the Bells
Sung to: "Frere Jacques"

^C
Merry Christmas, Merry Christmas,

Hear the bells, hear the bells.

Ringing in the season,

Ringing in the season.

^C
Ding, dong bells; ding, dong bells.

Bonnie Woodard
Shreveport, LA

Ring the Bells
Sung to: "Row, Row, Row Your Boat"

^C
Ring, ring, ring the bells,

Ring them loud and clear

To say to people everywhere

That ^GChristmastime is ^Chere.

Karen Vollmer
Wauseon, OH

Christmas Candles
Sung to: "Twinkle, Twinkle, Little Star"

C   F   C
Christmas candles burning bright,

G7   C   G7   C
Shining in the winter night.

       G7   C   G7
Shining there for all to see,

C   G7   C   G7
Christmas candles one, two, three.

C   F   C
Christmas candles burning bright,

G7   C   G7   C
Shine until the morning light.

To use this song for other celebrations, substitute the word "holiday" for "Christmas."

Bonnie Woodard
Shreveport, LA

Red, Green, White Christmas Colors
Sung to: "Three Blind Mice"

C G7 C   G7   C
Red, green, white; red, green, white,

    G7 C   G7 C
Christmas colors, Christmas colors.

       C7   C
Red is the color on holly wreaths,

       G7   C
Green is the color of Christmas trees,

       G7   C
White is the color from stars so bright.

      G7 C   G7   C
Red, green, white; red, green, white.

Deborah A. Roessel
Flemington, NJ

Christmas Song
Sung to: "I'm a Little Teapot"

C   F   C
I'm a little snowman, round and fat,

G7   C   G7   C
Here is my scarf and here is my hat.

                          F   C
When Christmas comes around just hear me shout,

          F   G7   C
"Here comes Santa. You better watch out!"

C   F   C
I'm a little light bulb, round and bright,

G7   C   G7   C
Here is my twinkle; oh, what a sight!

                         F   C
When Christmas comes around just plug me in,

         F   G7   C
And watch me blink again and again.

C   F
I'm a little Christmas tree, short and green,

G7   C   G7   C
Here are my branches, the cutest you've seen.

                    F   C
When I get all decorated, hear me cheer,

    F   G7   C
"Merry Christmas and Happy New Year!"

Vivian Sasser
Independence, MO

Christmas Sun
Sung to: "Jingle Bells"

We may not play in ^{F} snow

Or wear big heavy $^{B^b}$ clothes,

But everybody ^{C7} knows

What time of year is ^{F} near.

We decorate the tree

And light the candles $^{B^b}$ bright.

We sing this song and ^{F} clap our hands

^{C7} Because it's Christmas ^{F} night, oh —

^{F} Christmastime! Christmastime!

Christmastime is here!

^{C7} We have sun and ^{F} lots of fun

^{G7} When we have Christmas ^{C7} here!

^{F} Christmastime! Christmastime!

Christmastime is here!

^{C7} We have sun and ^{F} lots of fun

^{C7} When we have Christmas ^{F} here!

Nancy Nason Biddinger
Orlando, FL

A Sunny Christmas
Sung to: "Jack and Jill"

There is no ^{G} ice, ^{C}

There is no ^{G} snow, ^{C}

At ^{G} Christmastime in ^{C} Flor ^{G} ida.

But ^{Am} I can play

In the ^{G} sun all day,

^{Am} On Christmas ^{D7} Day in ^{G} Florida!

Substitute the name of your sunny city, town or state for "Florida."

Nancy Nason Biddinger
Orlando, FL

NEW YEAR'S DAY

A Brand New Year
Sung to: "The Muffin Man"

F
Now we have a brand new year,

  G7   C7
A brand new year, a brand new year.

F
Now we have a brand new year,

G7 C   F
It's <u>(name of year)</u>.

Neoma Kreuter
Ontario, CA

New Year's Day
Sung to: "Mary Had a Little Lamb"

     C
The old year's coming to an end,

G7   C
To an end, to an end.

Now a new year will begin.

G7
Happy New Year's Day!
               C

Sue Brown
Louisville, KY

It's a New Year
Sung to: "Frere Jacques"

C
It's a new year, it's a new year,

January first, January first.

Out with the old,

In with the new.

C
Happy New Year! Happy New Year!

C
Horns are tooting, horns are tooting,

January first, January first.

Throw some confetti,

Throw some confetti.

C
Happy New Year! Happy New Year!

Debra Lindahl
Libertyville, IL

Cheer the Year
Sung to: "Row, Row, Row Your Boat"

C
Cheer, cheer, cheer the year,

A new one's just begun.

Celebrate with all your friends,

G7   C
Let's go have some fun!

C
Clap, clap, clap your hands,

A brand new year is here.

Learning, laughing, singing, clapping,

G7   C
Through another year.

Susan Paprocki
Northbrook, IL

A New Year on Our Calendar
Sung to: "She'll Be Coming Round the Mountain"

          F
There's a new year on our calendar today.

  "(Name of year)!"

                           C7
There's a new year on our calendar today.

  "(Name of year)!"
          F
There's a new year on our calendar,

Bb
A year to grow and learn much more.

F   C7   F
There's a new year on our calendar today.

  "(Name of year)!"

Nancy Nason Biddinger
Orlando, FL

Let's Celebrate
Sung to: "Frere Jacques"

C
Happy New Year, Happy New Year,

Let's celebrate, let's celebrate.

Goodbye to the old year,

Hello to the new year.

C
Hurray, hurray! Hurray, hurray!

Patricia Coyne
Mansfield, MA

Happy New Year
Sung to: "Happy Birthday"

F C
Happy New Year to you,

F
Happy New Year to you.

B♭
May good times and good friends

F C F
Last the whole year through!

Betty Loew White
Amarillo, TX

Celebrate
Sung to: "Three Blind Mice"

C G7 C G7 C
Celebrate! Celebrate!

G7 C G7 C
A brand new year, a brand new year.

G7 C
Already it's time for another year,

G7 C
We hope it's filled with lots of good cheer,

G7 C
We'll grow bigger and better this year.

G7 C G7 C
Celebrate! Celebrate!

Additional verses: "Clap your hands; Stamp
your feet;" etc.

Susan Paprocki
Northbrook, IL

New Year's Here
Sung to: "Frere Jacques"

C
Crash your cymbals, toot your horns,

New Year's here! New Year's here!

A time for happy drumming,

New birthdays are coming.

C
New Year's Day! New Year's Day!

Betty Silkunas
Lansdale, PA

MARTIN LUTHER KING, JR.'S BIRTHDAY

Martin Luther King
Sung to: "Mary Had a Little Lamb"

C
Who was Martin Luther King,

G7   C
Luther King, Luther King?

He was a man who had a dream

     G7   C
That we would all be free.

C
Martin Luther gave a speech,

G7   C
Gave a speech, gave a speech.

He wanted all of us to live

  G7   C
In peace and harmony.

     C
He won the Nobel Prize for Peace,

G7   C
Prize for Peace, Prize for Peace,

For his love for all the world

G7   C
And for you and me.

Josette Brown
Bridgeport, WV

Brotherhood
Sung to: "Mary Had a Little Lamb"

C
Brotherhood for you and me,

G7   C
You and me, you and me.

Brotherhood for you and me,

      G7   C
Taught Martin Luther King.

C
We should live in harmony,

G7   C
Harmony, harmony.

We should live in harmony,

      G7   C
Taught Martin Luther King.

Debra Lindahl
Libertyville, IL

Martin Luther King Had a Dream
Sung to: "The Battle Hymn of the Republic"

G
Martin Luther King had a dream,

Yes, he did.
C   G
Martin Luther King had a dream,

Indeed, he did.

He dreamed we'd live as brothers

Having love for one another,
C   D7   G
And his dream is still alive through you and me.

Chorus:

G
Dr. King had a dream,
C   G
Dr. King had a dream.

Dr. King had a dream,
C   D7   G
And his dream is still alive through you and me.

G
Martin Luther King dreamed of peace

Among all men.
C   G
Martin Luther King dreamed of peace

Throughout the land.

No matter what our color,

Black or white or any other,
C   D7   G
We can live in peace together, yes, we can.

Chorus

Susan Paprocki
Northbrook, IL

He Dreamed of World Peace
Sung to: "The Muffin Man"

F
Do you know whose birthday's today,
G7   C7
Birthday's today, birthday's today?
F
Do you know whose birthday's today?
     G7   C   F
It's Martin Luther King's.

F
He dreamed of world peace,
G7   C7
Of world peace, of world peace.
F
He dreamed of world peace.
        G7   C   F
Let's honor him today!

Jean Warren

Dr. King
Sung to: "Yankee Doodle"

C   G7
Dr. King was a man
         C   G
Who had a special dream.
         C   F
He dreamed of a world filled with love
         G7   C
And peace and harmony.
F
Happy Birthday, Dr. King,
C
Happy Birthday to you.
F
Happy Birthday, Dr. King,
         C   G7   C
We love you, yes, we do.

Debra Butler
Denver, CO

GROUNDHOG DAY

Mr. Groundhog
Sung to: "Twinkle, Twinkle, Little Star"

C   F   C
Mr. Groundhog in the ground,

G7   C   G7 C
Pop your head up, look around.

       G7   C G7
Do you see your shadow?

C   G7   C   G7
Look up high and look down low.

C   F   C
Mr. Groundhog in the ground,

G7   C   G7 C
Pop your head up, look around.

Deborah A. Roessel
Flemington, NJ

Groundhog Song
Sung to: "Oh, My Darling Clementine"

   F
Mr. Groundhog, Mr. Groundhog,

           C7
Where are you today?

              F
Mr. Groundhog, Mr. Groundhog,

   C7   F
Are you coming out to play?

  F
If your shadow you do see,

           C7
Will you run away and hide?

         F
Then more days of winter

   C7   F
We'll expect to see outside.

June Meckel
Andover, MA

Here's a Little Groundhog
Sung to: "I'm a Little Teapot"

C   F   C
Here's a little groundhog, furry and brown.

G7   C   G7 C
He's coming up to look around.

                F   C
If he sees his shadow, down he'll go —

     F   G7   C
Then six more weeks of winter — oh, no!

Nancy Nason Biddinger
Orlando, FL

Nine Little Groundhogs
Sung to: "Ten Little Indians"

C
One little, two little, three little groundhogs,

G7
Four little, five little, six little groundhogs,

C
Seven little, eight little, nine little groundhogs,

G7   C
Sleeping down under the ground.

Have fun singing this song with loud voices, with "inside" voices, with whisper voices and then with "lip" voices (lips move but no sound comes out).

Colraine Pettipaw Hunley
Doylestown, PA

VALENTINE'S DAY

Special Friend
Sung to: "London Bridge"

My ^Cvalentine is red and white,

^{G7}Red and white, ^Cred and white.

My valentine is red and white.

It's ^{G7}for my special ^Cfriend.

^CCan you guess my special friend,

^{G7}Special friend, ^Cspecial friend?

Can you guess my special friend?

^{G7}Did you guess? It's ^Cyou!

Patricia Coyne
Mansfield, MA

Valentine's Day
Sung to: "Frere Jacques"

^CValentine's Day, Valentine's Day,

Time for fun, time for fun.

Sharing with our friends,

Sharing with our friends

^CCards of love, cards of love.

^CFriends forever, friends forever,

You and I, you and I.

I will be your good friend,

I will be your good friend.

^CPlease be mine, please be mine.

Susan Paprocki
Northbrook, IL

Love, Love, Love
Sung to: "Three Blind Mice"

C   G7 C   G7   C
Love, love, love; love, love, love,

     G7   C   G7   C
See how it grows, see how it grows.

       G7   C
I love my friends and they love me,

      G7   C
We love others and then, you see,

               G7   C
There's more than enough for a big family —

     G7 C   G7   C
Love, love, love; love, love, love.

Betty Swyers
Cuyahoga Falls, OH

Valentines Are Made to Share
Sung to: "Mary Had a Little Lamb"

C
Valentines are made to share,

G7   C
Made to share, made to share.

Valentines are made to share

G7   C
With my friends at school.

C
I made you a valentine,

G7   C
Valentine, valentine.

I made you a valentine

G7   C
That says I love you!

Sue Brown
Louisville, KY

I'm a Valentine for You

Sung to: "She'll Be Coming Round the Mountain"

I'm a teeny tiny valentine for you,
(Use a tiny, squeaky voice.)

I'm a teeny tiny valentine for you.

I'm a teeny tiny valentine,

I'm always yours, will you be mine?

I'm a teeny tiny valentine for you.

I'm a medium-sized valentine for you,
(Use normal voice.)

I'm a medium-sized valentine for you.

I'm a medium-sized valentine,

I'm not too big and that's just fine.

I'm a medium-sized valentine for you.

I'm a great big valentine for you,
(Use loud voice.)

I'm a great big valentine for you.

I'm a great big valentine,

And I will love you all the time.

I'm a great big valentine for you.

Nancy Nason Biddinger
Orlando, FL

I'm a Happy Little Heart

Sung to: "I'm a Little White Duck"

I'm a happy little heart

That's pink and white and red.

A happy little heart

With lace around my edge.

I have three words

On the front of me.

That say I love you,

Oh, can't you see?

I'm a happy little heart

That's pink and white and red.

Happy little heart.

Gayle Bittinger

Here's a Valentine Just for You
Sung to: "Frere Jacques"

C
Here's a valentine, here's a valentine,

Just for you, just for you.

It has hearts and roses,

It has hearts and roses.

C
Kisses, too; kisses, too.

Barbara Paxson
Warren, OH

Valentines I've Made for You
Sung to: "Twinkle, Twinkle, Little Star"

C   F   C
Valentines I've made for you,

G7   C   G7   C
Some with hearts and flowers, too.

    G7   C   G7
All of them bring love from me,

C   G7   C   G7
Each one's special, you will see.

C   F   C
If you promise to be mine,

G7   C   G7 C
I'll give you my valentines.

Maureen Gutyan
Williams Lake, B.C.

I Made a Big Red Lacy Heart
Sung to: "Bingo"

  F   Bb F
I made a big red lacy heart,

      C   F
That I will give to you.

         Bb
Here is your valentine,

C   F
Here is your valentine,

         Bb
Here is your valentine,

  C   F
I like you, yes, I do!

Maureen Gutyan
Williams Lake, B.C.

Lacy Hearts
Sung to: "Jingle Bells"

F
Lacy hearts, candy hearts,

Flowery hearts, too.

C7   F
Hearts of pink, hearts of yellow,

G7   C7
Hearts of red and blue.

F
Lacy hearts, candy hearts,

Flowery hearts, too.

C7   F
Oh, what fun it is to share

C7   F
Lots of hearts with you!

Betty Silkunas
Lansdale, PA

I Get Valentines
Sung to: "The Farmer in the Dell"

C
I get valentines

From all my special friends.

I love to get, I love to give

C   G7   C
Valentines today.

Patricia Coyne
Mansfield, MA

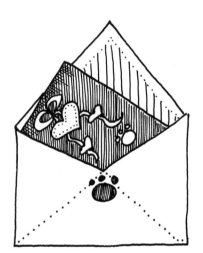

These Red Valentines
Sung to: "She'll Be Coming Round the Mountain"

F
These red valentines all say that I love you,

                                    C7
These red valentines all say that I love you.

            F
These red valentines all say,

            B♭
These red valentines all say,

            F   C7   F
These red valentines all say that I love you.

Betty Silkunas
Lansdale, PA

A Valentine Song for You
Sung to: "If You're Happy and You Know It"

Oh, this valentine song is for you!
G D

I don't need crayons, scissors or some glue!
G

Yes, this little song I'll sing,
C

Hugs and kisses it will bring.
G

Oh, this valentine song is for you!
D G

Becky Valenick
Mesa, AZ

Hearts and Flowers
Sung to: "Oh, My Darling Clementine"

Valentine, Valentine,
F

Valentine, will you be mine?
C7

I will be your friend forever,
F

If you'll be my valentine.
C7   F

Hearts and flowers, hearts and flowers,
F

Hearts and flowers I will send.
C7

If you'll only be mine,
F

Hearts and flowers I will send.
C7   F

Gayle Bittinger

Here Is a Valentine
Sung to: "You Are My Sunshine"

Here is a valentine, a great big valentine,
F

I made it special just for you.
Bb   F

It's red and lacy with lots of kisses.
Bb   F

It's for you 'cause you're my friend.
C7   F

Maureen Gutyan
Williams Lake, B.C.

Big Red Hearts
Sung to: "Frere Jacques"

C
Big red hearts, big red hearts,

Made with lace, made with lace.

Sent with love and kisses,

Sent with love and kisses
C
To our friends, to our friends.

Maureen Gutyan
Williams Lake, B.C.

Be My Valentine
Sung to: "Mary Had a Little Lamb"

C
You're a special friend of mine,

G7   C
Friend of mine, friend of mine.

You're a special friend of mine.

G7   C
Be my valentine!

Jean Warren

Valentines Say I Love You
Sung to: "London Bridge"

C
Valentines say I love you,

G7   C
I love you, I love you.

Valentines say I love you.

G7   C
Yes, I really do.

Bonnie Woodard
Shreveport, LA

I've Got a Big Red Heart
Sung to: "For He's a Jolly Good Fellow"

^F
I've got a big red ^{B♭}heart^F

That ^CI will give to ^Fyou.

It brings you love and ^{B♭}kisses,

Be^Ccause you ^{B♭}are ^Cmy ^Ffriend.

Maureen Gutyan
Williams Lake, B.C.

Yes, This Is a Special Day
Sung to: "Oh Dear, What Can the Matter Be?

^C
Yes, yes, this is a special day,

^{G7}
Yes, yes, this is a special day,

^C
Yes, yes, this is a special day,

^{G7}
I can give hearts to my ^Cfriends.

Susan Peters
Upland, CA

H-E-A-R-T
Sung to: "Bingo"

^F
To show you like your ^{B♭}special ^Ffriends,

Just give them ^Ceach a ^Fheart.

^FH-^{B♭}E-A-^CR-^FT, H-E-A-R-T, H-E-A-R-T,^{B♭}

Each heart ^Csays I like ^Fyou!

Debra Lindahl
Libertyville, IL

I'll Make a Valentine
Sung to: "London Bridge"

I'll make a bright red valentine, [C]

Valentine, [G7] valentine. [C]

I'll make a bright red valentine,

And give it [G7] right to [C] you.

I'll trim it [C] with lace and bows,

Lace and [G7] bows, lace and [C] bows.

I'll trim it with lace and bows,

And give it [G7] right to [C] you.

Elizabeth Vollrath
Stevens Pt., WI

Three Valentines
Sung to: "Mary Had a Little Lamb"

Three [C] valentines I have for you,

Have for [G7] you, have for [C] you.

Three valentines I have for you,

Pink and [G7] red and [C] blue.

I'll [C] put them in the mail for you,

Mail for [G7] you, mail for [C] you.

I'll put them in the mail for you,

Pink and [G7] red and [C] blue.

Gayle Bittinger

February
Sung to: "Frere Jacques"

This is [C] February, this is February.

Groundhog Day, Valentine's,

Lincoln's birthday,

Washington's, too.

Wintertime, [C] wintertime.

Debbie Zanaty
Birmingham, AL

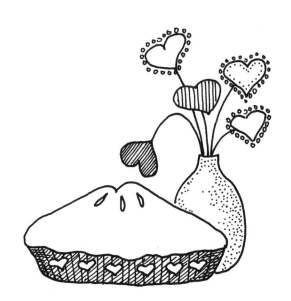

ABRAHAM LINCOLN'S BIRTHDAY

Abraham Lincoln
Sung to: "The Battle Hymn of the Republic"

G
Abraham Lincoln

Was the President, you know.

C
He led our land, America,

   G
A long, long time ago.

He worked to put an end to war,

He worked to make men free.
      D7   G
That's why we all remember him, you see.

Vicki Claybrook
Kennewick, WA

Lincoln
Sung to: "Mary Had a Little Lamb"

C
Lincoln lived in a log cabin,

  G7   C
A log cabin, a log cabin.

Lincoln lived in a log cabin,

G7   C
As a little boy.

C
Lincoln was the President,

G7   C
President, President.

Lincoln was the President

G7   C
Of America.

Bonnie Woodard
Shreveport, LA

A Great Man
Sung to: "Twinkle, Twinkle, Little Star"

C   F   C
A great man you ought to know,

G7   C   G7   C
Lived a long, long time ago.

           G7   C G7
Abraham Lincoln, the President,

C   G7   C G7
Gave freedom to each resident.

     C   F   C
He made the world a better place

   G7   C   G7   C
For you and me and the human race.

Carol Metzker
Oregon, OH

Lincoln Was Our President
Sung to: "Pop! Goes the Weasel"

C   G   C
Abraham Lincoln was a man

           G   C
Who set the people free.

         G   C
He wore a tall hat and had a dark beard,

   F   G   C
Our President was he.

       G   C
All around the country,

            G C
The people were at war.

       G   C
Lincoln helped to save our land

    F G   C
And so much more.

Barbara Paxson
Warren, OH

Lincoln's Birthday Song
Sung to: "The Muffin Man"

F
Do you know whose birthday's today,

G7   C7
Birthday's today, birthday's today?

F
Do you know whose birthday's today?

G7 C   F
It's Abraham Lincoln's.

      F
He wanted all people to be free,

G7   C7
To be free, to be free.

     F
He wanted all people to be free.

G7   C F
Let's honor him today.

Jean Warren

Thank You, Mr. Lincoln
Sung to: "Yankee Doodle"

C   G7
Lincoln was our President,

C   G
He was very honest.

     C   F
He cared for all, both black and white,

  G7   C
He tried to help all people.

F
Abraham Lincoln, you were brave,

      C
You made all people free.

     F
You always did what you thought best.

C   G7 C
Thank you, Mr. Lincoln.

Patricia Coyne
Mansfield, MA

GEORGE WASHINGTON'S BIRTHDAY

Washington's Birthday Song
Sung to: "The Muffin Man"

F
Do you know whose birthday's today,

G7   C7
Birthday's today, birthday's today?

F
Do you know whose birthday's today?

    G7   C   F
It's George Washington's.

F
He was America's first President,

G7   C7
First president, first President.

F
He was America's first President,

      G7 C   F
Let's honor him today.

Jean Warren

George Washington
Sung to: "Yankee Doodle"

          C
George Washington was the first

        G7 C   G
President of our country.

        C   F
The people loved him, one and all,

    G7   C
He worked to make our land free.

    F
He led the soldiers — that was hard,

        C
For they were cold and hungry.

    F
He said, "Be brave, now don't give up.

        C   G7   C
We'll build a brand new country."

Vicki Claybrook
Kennewick, WA

Whose Fine Face?
Sung to: "London Bridge"

C
Whose fine face is on the penny,

G7   C
On the penny, on the penny?

Whose fine face is on the penny?

G7   C
Abraham Lincoln's.

C
Whose fine face is on the quarter,

G7   C
On the quarter, on the quarter?

Whose fine face is on the quarter?

G7   C
George Washington's.

Betty Silkunas
Lansdale, PA

Our First President
Sung to: "Ten Little Indians"

C
George Washington was our President,

G7
George Washington was our President.

C
He was the first President,

G   C
George Washington.

C
He was a hero to the people,

G7
He was a hero to the people.

C
He helped our country win its freedom,

G   C
George Washington.

Patricia Coyne
Mansfield, MA

 Spring

St. Patrick's Day Is Here
Sung to: "The Farmer in the Dell"

St. Patrick's Day is here,
$\overset{C}{\text{St.}}$

St. Patrick's Day is here.

Let's give a clap and dance a jig,

St. Patrick's Day is here.

JoAnn C. Leist
Smithfield, NC

Catch Him If You Can
Sung to: "The Muffin Man"

Oh, have you seen a leprechaun,

A leprechaun, a leprechaun?

Oh, have you seen a leprechaun,

Who comes from Ireland?

Among the shamrocks he may hide,

He may hide, he may hide.

Among the shamrocks he may hide,

So catch him if you can.

Maureen Gutyan
Williams Lake, B.C.

I'm an Irish Leprechaun
Sung to: "I'm a Little Teapot"

I'm an Irish leprechaun,

Tiny and wee,

I hide in the forest,

Behind a tree.

If you ever catch me, you will see

A wish I'll grant as quick as can be.

Maureen Gutyan
Williams Lake, B.C.

Eensy, Weensy Leprechaun
Sung to: "Eensy, Weensy Spider"

An eensy, weensy leprechaun
F

Came out St. Patrick's Day
C7   F

To look for the gold

That was hidden far away.
C7   F

Over the rainbow

Was where he was told,
C7   F

So, with a wink of his green eye,

He ran to get the gold.
C7   F

Sharon Smith
Doylestown, PA

Paddy Is His Name
Sung to: "Bingo"

I know a tiny little man
F   B♭ F

Who dresses all in green.
C F

He is a leprechaun,
B♭

He is a leprechaun,
C F

He is a leprechaun,
B♭

And Paddy is his name.
C   F

He lives across the ocean wide,
F   B♭ F

He's rarely ever seen.
C F

He is a leprechaun,
B♭

He is a leprechaun,
C F

He is a leprechaun,
B♭

And Paddy is his name.
C   F

Maureen Gutyan
Williams Lake, B.C.

I'm a Little Leprechaun
Sung to: "I'm a Little Teapot"

C
I'm a little leprechaun

F   C
Dressed in green,

   G7   C
The tiniest man

     G7   C
That you have ever seen.

                        F   C
If you ever catch me, so it's told,

      F   G7   C
I'll give you my pot of gold.

Vicki Claybrook
Kennewick, WA

I Saw a Leprechaun
Sung to: "If You're Happy and You Know It"

 G   D
I saw a leprechaun yesterday,

 D   G
I saw a leprechaun yesterday.

        C
Yes, I saw him yesterday,

        G
Going on his merry way.

       D   G
With a twinkle in his eye, he said, "Good day!"

Barbara Paxson
Warren, OH

I'm a Tiny Little Green Man
Sung to: "Ten Little Indians"

C
I'm a tiny little green man,

G7
I'm a tiny little green man,

C
I'm a tiny little green man,

      G7   C
I'm called a leprechaun.

C
I run and hide among the trees,

G7
I run and hide among the trees,

C
I run and hide among the trees,

    G7   C
I'm hardly ever seen.

C
If you spy me, I'll grant your wish,

G7
If you spy me, I'll grant your wish,

C
If you spy me, I'll grant your wish,

          G7   C
Good luck I'll bring to you.

Maureen Gutyan
Williams Lake, B.C.

APRIL FOOL'S DAY

April Fool's Day
Sung to: "Jingle Bells"

F
April Fool's, April Fool's,

What a lot of fun.

C7   F
Everyone is playing tricks

    G7   C7
On each and every one.

F
Men from Mars, falling stars,

Big black bugs and more.

C7   F
You trick me, I trick you,

          C7   F
That's what April Fool's is for.

Jean Warren

All Around the Town Today
Sung to: "Pop! Goes the Weasel"

C   G   C
All around the town today,

    G   C
Even here at school,

     G   C
Everyone is playing tricks.

F   G   C
Surprise! It's April Fool's!

Jean Warren

Giant, Giant Spider
Sung to: "Eensy, Weensy Spider"

F
Giant, giant spider,

C7   F
Crawling up your back.

F
Here, let me help you

C7   F
Give your back a whack.

It was very ugly,

    C7   F
So very mean and cruel.

Aren't you glad I saved you?

C7   F
Happy April Fool!

Jean Warren

EASTER

Eastertime
Sung to: "Row, Row, Row Your Boat"

C
It is Eastertime,

Bunnies, touch your knees.

Clap your hands and tap your toes,
G   C
Please join in with me.

**Joyce Hamman
Dana Point, CA**

Easter, Easter
Sung to: "Sailing, Sailing"

C   F   C
Easter, Easter, Eastertime is here.

     G7   C
We'll decorate some hard-boiled eggs

   D   G7
And hide them, yes, my dear!

C   F   C
Bunnies, baskets, new clothes everywhere —

     G7   C
We'll sing and dance and wear our hats

    D   G   C
'Cause Eastertime is here!

**Colraine Pettipaw Hunley
Doylestown, PA**

It Is Easter
Sung to: "Frere Jacques"

C
It is Easter, it is Easter.

Bunnies are jumping all around.

Their paws touch the ground,

As they bounce around.

C
Eastertime, Eastertime.

**Joyce Hamman
Dana Point, CA**

Let Us Sing an Easter Song
Sung to: "Mary Had a Little Lamb"

C
Let us sing an Easter song,

G7   C
Easter song, Easter song.

Let us sing an Easter song.

G7   C
Happy, Happy Easter!

C
Easter's such a happy day,

G7   C
Happy day, happy day.

Easter's such a happy day.

G7   C
Happy, Happy Easter!

Karen Vollmer
Wauseon, OH

A Happy Easter
Sung to: "Twinkle, Twinkle, Little Star"

C   F   C
Eastertime is full of cheer,

G7   C   G7 C
It means spring is really here.

         G7   C   G7
Baskets, flowers and fancy hats,

C   G7 C   G7
Rabbits, too, remember that!

      C   F   C
So all I really want to say

G7   C   G7   C
Is have a Happy Easter Day!

Becky Valenick
Mesa, AZ

So Early Easter Morning
Sung to: "The Mulberry Bush"

D
This is the way we hold the basket,

A7
Hold the basket, hold the basket.

D
This is the way we hold the basket,

    A7   D
So early Easter morning.

D
This is the way we hunt for eggs,

A7
Hunt for eggs, hunt for eggs.

D
This is the way we hunt for eggs,

    A7   D
So early Easter morning.

D
This is the way we find the eggs,

A7
Find the eggs, find the eggs.

D
This is the way we find the eggs,

    A7   D
So early Easter morning.

D
This is the way we eat the eggs,

A7
Eat the eggs, eat the eggs.

D
This is the way we eat the eggs,

    A7   D
So early Easter morning.

Debra Lindahl
Libertyville, IL

Easter Eggs
Sung to: "Jingle Bells"

F
Easter eggs, Easter eggs,

Eggs of orange and blue.

C7   F
Here are lots of colored eggs

G7   C7
All for me and you.

F
Chocolate eggs colored brown,

Jelly beans bright green.

C7   F
Aren't these the most beautiful eggs

    C7   F
That you have ever seen?

Maureen Gutyan
Williams Lake, B.C.

Peter the Easter Bunny
Sung to: "Rudolph the Red-Nosed Reindeer"

C
Peter the Easter Bunny

            G7
Has a basket full of eggs.

Peter the Easter Bunny

          C
Has the fastest bunny legs.

Peter the Easter Bunny

          G7
Visits little girls and boys.

Peter the Easter Bunny

          C
Brings us lots of Easter joys.

F   C   C7
Just wake up on Easter Day,

Dm   G7 C
Tiptoe down the stairs.

G
Peter with the fastest legs

    Am   D7   G
Will have left your treats right there.

   C
Oh, Peter the Easter Bunny

           G7
Has a basket full of eggs.

Peter the Easter Bunny

          C
Has the fastest bunny legs.

Betty Silkunas
Lansdale, PA

Easter Bunny Hops Along
Sung to: "Yankee Doodle"

C   G7
Easter Bunny hops along,

C   G
Easter's here again.

      C   F
He's painted many colored eggs

G7   C
To give to all his friends.

F
Easter Bunny hops along,

     C
He hides his colored eggs.

F
Easter Bunny hops along,

    C   G7   C
It's Eastertime again.

Maureen Gutyan
Williams Lake, B.C.

I'm a Little Chicken
Sung to: "I'm a Little Teapot"

C
I'm a little chicken,

F   C
Ready to hatch,

G7   C
Pecking at my shell,

G7   C
Scratch, scratch, scratch.

               F   C
When I crack it open, out I'll leap,

        F   G7   C
Fluff up my feathers and cheep, cheep, cheep!

Susan Peters
Upland, CA

Bunny-Pokey
Sung to: "Hokey-Pokey"

C
You put your bunny ears in,
   (Place hands on head to make "ears.")

You put your bunny ears out,

You put your bunny ears in,

G
And you shake them all about.

You do the Bunny-Pokey,

And you hop yourself around —

C
That's what it's all about!

C
You put your bunny nose in,
   (Wiggle nose.)

You put your bunny nose out,

You put your bunny nose in,

G
And you shake it all about.

You do the Bunny-Pokey,

And you hop yourself around —

C
That's what it's all about!

C
You put your bunny tail in,
   (Wiggle hips.)

You put your bunny tail out,

You put your bunny tail in,

G
And you shake it all about.

You do the Bunny-Pokey,

And you hop yourself around —

C
That's what it's all about!

Betty Silkunas
Lansdale, PA

I'm a Little Bunny
Sung to: "I'm a Little Teapot"

C   F   C
I'm a little bunny with a cotton tail,

G7   C   G7   C
See me hop down the bunny trail.
   (Hop down a pretend lane.)

C   F   C
When I spy a carrot, my ears they shake,
   (Put hands up behind head and shake them.)

          F   G7   C
Then, of course, a bite I take. "Crunch!"
   (Pretend to bite carrot.)

Joy M. Zomerdyke
Freehold, NJ

Like a Bunny Would
Sung to: "Row, Row, Row Your Boat"

C
Flop, flop, flop your ears,

Flop them up and down.

Flop, flop, flop your ears,
G   C
Like a bunny would.

C
Wiggle, wiggle, wiggle your nose,

Wiggle it all around.

Wiggle, wiggle, wiggle your nose,
G   C
Like a bunny would.

C
Shake, shake, shake your tail,

Shake it back and forth.

Shake, shake, shake your tail,
G   C
Like a bunny would.

C
Hop, hop, up and down,

Hop all down the lane.

Hop, hop, up and down,
G   C
Like a bunny would.

Peggy Wolf
Pittsburgh, PA

One Easter Rabbit
Sung to: "The ABC Song"

C
One Easter Rabbit hopped away
   G7   C
To hide the Easter eggs one day.

He said, "This job I'll never get done,
   G7   C
If I don't call another rabbit to come."

C
Two Easter Rabbits hopped away
   G7   C
To hide the Easter eggs one day.

They said, "This job we'll never get done,
   G7   C
If we don't call another rabbit to come."

C
(Eight/Nine/etc.) Easter Rabbits hopped away
   G7   C
To hide the Easter eggs one day.

They had such enormous fun,
   G7   C
But they were glad their job was done.

Select a child to be the first Easter Rabbit. At the end of the second verse, select another child to join the first rabbit. Continue until all the children have been chosen.

Ellen Javernick
Loveland, CO

Joe the Bunny
Sung to: "I'm a Little Teapot"

C   F   C
I'm a little bunny, my name is Joe.
(Hold up two fingers.)

G7   C   G7   C
I hop fast and I hop slow.
(Hop fingers around fast and slow.)

C   F   C
Whenever I get sleepy, my ears droop low,
(Bend fingers down.)

      F   G7   C
But after my nap, up they go!
(Hold fingers straight up.)

Karen L. Brown
Bentonville, AR

B-U-N-N-Y
Sung to: "Old MacDonald Had a Farm"

F   Bb   F
Who wiggles his nose, twitch, twitch, twitch?

    C7   F
B-U-N-N-Y!

              Bb   F
Who flops his ears, swish, swish, swish?

    C7   F
B-U-N-N-Y!

He's bringing eggs, his baskets are filled,

He knows the children will be thrilled.

              Bb   F
Who moves this way, hop, hop, hop?

    C7   F
B-U-N-N-Y!

Debra Lindahl
Libertyville, IL

I'm an Easter Bunny
Sung to: "I'm a Little Teapot"

C   F   C
I'm an Easter Bunny, watch me hop,

G7   C   G7   C
Here are my two ears, see how they flop.

             F   C
I'm a happy fellow, here's my nose,

     F   G7   C
I'm all furry from my head to my toes.

C   F   C
I bring Easter goodies to your house,

G7   C   G7   C
Carrying my baskets, quiet as a mouse.

                    F   C
Jelly beans and chocolates, colored eggs, too,

     F   G7   C
Easter Bunny yummies, just for you.

Susan Paprocki
Northbrook, IL

Three Easter Bunnies
Sung to: "Three Blind Mice"

C   G7   C   G7   C
Three Easter Bunnies, three Easter Bunnies,

   G7   C   G7   C
Hip, hip, hop; hip, hip, hop.

             G7   C
With baskets full, they hop around,

              G7   C
They hide their Easter eggs on the ground,

         G7   C
Then hop away without a sound.

   G7   C   G7   C
Hip, hip, hop; hip, hip, hop.

Betty Silkunas
Lansdale, PA

Easter Rabbit
Sung to: "Frere Jacques"

C
Easter Rabbit, Easter Rabbit,

Here he comes, here he comes.

Hiding Easter eggs,

Hiding Easter eggs.

C
Oh, what fun! Oh, what fun!

Bonnie Woodard
Shreveport, LA

Little Bunny
Sung to: "Twinkle, Twinkle, Little Star"

C   F   C
Little Bunny, turn around,

G7   C   G7   C
Little Bunny, touch the ground.

    G7   C   G7
Little Bunny, wiggle your nose,

C   G7   C   G7
Little Bunny, touch your toes.

C   F   C
Little Bunny, rest your head,

G7   C   G7   C
Little Bunny, jump in bed.

Joy M. Zomerdyke
Freehold, NJ

Have You Seen the Easter Bunny?
Sung to: "The Muffin Man"

F
Have you seen the Easter Bunny,

    G7   C7
With cotton tail and ears so funny?

F
Have you seen the Easter Bunny?

G7   C   F
Hop, hop, hippity hop!

Betty Silkunas
Lansdale, PA

I Know a Rabbit
Sung to: "Bingo"

  F   B♭   F
I know a rabbit with long pink ears,

           C   F
And Bunny is his name-o.

      B♭   C   F   B♭
B-U-N-N-Y, B-U-N-N-Y, B-U-N-N-Y,

           C   F
And Bunny is his name-o.

     F   B♭   F
He hops to your house on Easter morn,

           C   F
And Bunny is his name-o.

      B♭   C   F   B♭
B-U-N-N-Y, B-U-N-N-Y, B-U-N-N-Y,

           C   F
And Bunny is his name-o.

      F   B♭   F
He hides colored eggs around your yard,

        F   C   F
And Bunny is his name-o.

      B♭   C   F   B♭
B-U-N-N-Y, B-U-N-N-Y, B-U-N-N-Y,

           C   F
And Bunny is his name-o.

Karen Pound
Webster City, IA

MAY DAY

Ring Around the Maypole
Sung to: "Ring Around the Rosie"

C
Ring around the Maypole,

Pocket full of roses.

Ribbons, ribbons,

C
We all fall down!

Let the children take turns naming other soft things to fall into, such as "water, feathers, peanut butter, pillows," etc.

Toni Lenhardt
Cannon Beach, OR

May Is Here
Sung to: "Frere Jacques"

C
I see daisies, I see daisies,

Bloom in May, bloom in May.

May's the month for flowers,

Goodbye, April showers.

C
May is here, May is here.

Repeat, using names of other flowers that the children can see in May.

Betty Silkunas
Lansdale, PA

Hurray for May Day!
Sung to: "London Bridge"

C
May Day's here with sun so bright,

G7   C
Sun so bright, sun so bright.

May Day's here with sun so bright.

G7   C
Hurray for May Day!

C
May Day's here with flowers in bloom,

G7   C
Flowers in bloom, flowers in bloom.

May Day's here with flowers in bloom.

G7   C
Hurray for May Day!

Gayle Bittinger

MOTHER'S DAY

It's Your Special Day
Sung to: "The Muffin Man"

F
Mommy, it's your special day,

G7   C7
And it's time for me to say

   F
I'm glad for all the things you do.

G7   C   F
Thank you, Mommy, I love you!

Sue Brown
Louisville, KY

Mommy Takes Good Care of Me
Sung to: "Mary Had a Little Lamb"

C
Mommy takes good care of me,

G7   C
Care of me, care of me.

Mommy takes good care of me,

  G7   C
Because she loves me so.

Sue Brown
Louisville, KY

Happy Mother's Day to You
Sung to: "Mary Had a Little Lamb"

C
Happy Mother's Day to you,
G7   C
Day to you, Day to you.

Happy Mother's Day to you,
  G7   C
Oh, have a happy day!

C
This day was made just for you,
G7   C
Just for you, just for you.

This day was made just for you,
G7   C
Happy Mother's Day!

  C
I have a kiss and a hug for you,
G7   C
Hug for you, hug for you.

I have a kiss and a hug for you,
G7   C
And I love you, too!

Saundra Winnett
Lewisville, TX

You Are My Mother
Sung to: "You Are My Sunshine"

Chorus:
       F
You are my mother, my dear, dear mother,
     Bᵇ   F
You show you love me every day.
     Bᵇ   F
You give me hugs, you give me kisses,
      C   F
Please know I love you in every way!

       F
You think I'm special, so very special,
      Bᵇ   F
You're glad you have me as your child.
      Bᵇ   F
You read me stories and teach me lessons,
      C   F
Please know I love you in every way.

Chorus

       F
Sometimes you get mad, sometimes I get mad,
     Bᵇ F
We love each other just the same.
     Bᵇ   F
We forgive each other, we say we're sorry,
      C F
Please know I love you in every way.

Chorus

Debra Lindahl
Libertyville, IL

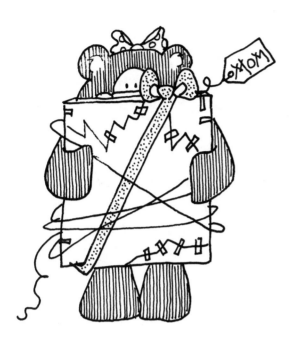

Mom Says
Sung to: "Twinkle, Twinkle, Little Star"

C   F   C
Sometimes Mom says, "Don't do this."

G7   C   G7   C
Sometimes Mom says, "Don't do that."

         G7   C   G7
She still loves me, that I know.

C   G7   C   G7
Why? Because she tells me so.

C   F   C
Sometimes Mom says, "Let's do this!"

G7   C   G7   C
Sometimes Mom says, "Kiss, kiss, kiss!"

Becky Valenick
Mesa, AZ

Mommy Is My Special Friend
Sung to: "Mary Had a Little Lamb"

C
Mommy is my special friend,

G7   C
Special friend, special friend.

Mommy is my special friend.

  G7   C
I like the things we do.

C
Mom and I have lots of fun,

G7   C
Lots of fun, lots of fun.

Mom and I have lots of fun.

  G7   C
I like to be with her.

Sue Brown
Louisville, KY

Three Kisses for Mother
Sung to: "Did You Ever See a Lassie?"

F
Three kisses for Mother,

     C7   F
For Mother, for Mother.

Three kisses for Mother,

   C7   F
It's her special day.

   C7   F
It's her special day,

   C7   F
It's her special day.

Three kisses for Mother,

   C7   F
It's her special day.

Betty Silkunas
Lansdale, PA

A Mom's a Special Lady
Sung to: "Eensy, Weensy Spider"

A mom's a special lady,
[F above "A"]

So hug her every day.
[C7 above "hug", F above "every"]

She gives you lots of food to eat,

And takes you out to play.
[C7 above "takes", F above "out"]

Your mother reads you stories,

And buys you sneakers, too.
[C7 above "buys", F above "sneakers"]

Aren't you happy that you have

A mom who loves you so?
[C7 above "mom", F above "loves"]

Betty Silkunas
Lansdale, PA

Thank You, Mom!
Sung to: "London Bridge"

Thank you, Mom, for all your hugs,
[C above "Thank"]

All your hugs, all your hugs.
[G7 above "All", C above "all"]

Thank you, Mom, for all your hugs.

They feel good to me.
[G7 above "They", C above "to"]

Thank you, Mom, for all your kisses,
[C above "Thank"]

All your kisses, all your kisses.
[G7 above "All", C above "all"]

Thank you, Mom, for all your kisses.

They feel good to me.
[G7 above "They", C above "to"]

Thank you, Mom, for all your love,
[C above "Thank"]

All your love, all your love.
[G7 above "All", C above "all"]

Thank you, Mom, for all your love.

It feels good to me.
[G7 above "It", C above "to"]

Becky Valenick
Mesa, AZ

Pick the Flowers
Sung to: "Frere Jacques"

C
Pick the flowers, pick the flowers,

One by one, one by one.

We'll give them to Mother,

We'll give them to Mother,

C
When we're done, when we're done.

Barbara Paxson
Warren, OH

Mother's Day Song
Sung to: "Frere Jacques"

C
We love mothers, we love mothers,

Yes, we do; yes, we do.

Mothers are for hugging,
(Hug self.)

Mothers are for kissing.
(Blow a kiss.)

C
We love you; yes, we do.

C
Thank you, mothers; thank you, mothers,

For your love, for your love.

Mothers are for hugging,
(Hug self.)

Mothers are for kissing.
(Blow a kiss.)

C
We love you; yes, we do.

Barbara Fletcher
El Cajon, CA

I Love Mommy
Sung to: "Frere Jacques"

C
I love Mommy, I love Mommy.

Yes, I do; yes, I do.

And my mommy loves me,

Yes, my mommy loves me,

C
Loves me, too; loves me, too.

Carla C. Skjong
Tyler, MN

I Love You, Mom
Sung to: "Frere Jacques"

C
I love you, Mom; I love you, Mom.

Yes, I do; yes, I do.

You are very special,

You are very special.

C
I love you; yes, I do.

Bonnie Woodard
Shreveport, LA

Mommy, Mommy
Sung to: "Sailing, Sailing"

C   F   C
Mommy, Mommy, here are my gifts to you.

    G7   C
A special hug and a kiss today

D   G7
Are my gifts to you.

    C   F   C
You always love me even when I'm bad.

    G7   C
You always find the time to care,

    D   G   C
You never leave me sad.

Patricia Coyne
Mansfield, MA

Additional songs for Mother's Day may be adapted from the Father's Day songs on pages 78 to 82.

 Summer

Father's Day
Sung to: "Oh, Christmas Tree"

Oh, Father's Day; oh, Father's Day,
G   D G

What a grand day it is.
Am   D7 G

Oh, Father's Day; oh, Father's Day,
D G

Honor Dad with love.
Am   D7   G

Give him hugs, love him true.
C   D7

Honor him with special you.
G

Oh, Father's Day; oh, Father's Day,
D G

We love you, yes, we do!
D   G

Kristine Wagoner
Pacific, WA

Happy Father's Day to You
Sung to: "Mary Had a Little Lamb"

Happy Father's Day to you,
C

Day to you, Day to you.
G7   C

I hope you know that I love you.

Happy Father's Day!
G7   C

Saundra Winnett
Lewisville, TX

D-A-D
Sung to: "Jingle Bells"

F
D-A-D, D-A-D,

Dad is my best friend.

C7   F
We play games, we go to the park,

G7   C7
The fun just never ends!

F
D-A-D, D-A-D,

I love to hold your hand.

C7   F
It feels so good, it feels so safe,

             C7   F
You're the best dad in this land!

Debra Lindahl
Libertyville, IL

My Special Friend
Sung to: "Yankee Doodle"

C   G7
Daddy is my special friend,

        C   G
The two of us are buddies.

        C   F
I always like the things we do,

        G7   C
I'm thankful for my daddy.

Sue Brown
Louisville, KY

Thank You, Dad
Sung to: "Row, Row, Row Your Boat"

C
Thanks, thanks, thank you, Dad,

Thanks for loving me!

Hugs and kisses, hugs and kisses,

G   C
Come to you from me!

Becky Valenick
Mesa, AZ

Gifts for Dad
Sung to: "The Muffin Man"

F
What gifts can I give my dad,

G7   C7
Give my dad, give my dad?

F
What gifts can I give my dad

G7 C F
For a Happy Father's Day?

  F
I know what I'll give my dad,

G7   C7
Give my dad, give my dad.

  F
I know what I'll give my dad,

G7   C F
Hugs and kisses today.

Patricia Coyne
Mansfield, MA

I Love Daddy
Sung to: "Frere Jacques"

C
I love Daddy, I love Daddy.

Yes, I do; yes, I do.

And my daddy loves me,

And my daddy loves me.

C
Loves me, too; loves me, too.

Carla C. Skjong
Tyler, MN

The Daddy Song
Sung to: "Pop! Goes the Weasel"

 C   G   C
I love to snuggle in my daddy's lap,

       G   C
And squeeze him tight like this.
  (Hug self.)

      G C
I love to tell him, "I love you so,"
  (Make kissing sound.)

F   G   C
With a great big kiss.

Vicki Claybrook
Kennewick, WA

He Is Very Special
Sung to: "Frere Jacques"

C
I love Daddy, I love Daddy.

Yes, I do; yes, I do.

He is very special,

He is very special.

C
I love him; yes, I do.

Bonnie Woodard
Shreveport, LA

Oh, My Daddy
Sung to: "Oh, My Darling Clementine"

      F   F
Oh, my daddy; oh, my daddy,

                   C7
Oh, my very special dad,

                        F
I want to thank you very much

         C7   F
For being my special dad.

Patricia Coyne
Mansfield, MA

Best Dad
Sung to: "This Old Man"

C
Father's Day, Father's Day,

F   G
Is a very special day.

        C
Here's a great big hug and lots of kisses, too.

G   C G C
Each one says that I love you!

Susan Peters
Upland, CA

Hugs for Daddy
Sung to: "Ten Little Indians"

C
One little, two little, three little hugs,

G7
Four little, five little, six little hugs,

C
Seven little, eight little, nine little hugs,

G7   C
Ten little hugs for Daddy.

C
One big, two big, three big hugs,

G7
Four big, five big, six big hugs,

C
Seven big, eight big, nine big hugs,

G7   C
Ten big hugs for Daddy.

**Betty Silkunas
Lansdale, PA**

Father Dear
Sung to: "Jingle Bells"

F
Father's Day, Father's Day,

It is almost here.

C7   F
It's the time when we say,

  G7   C7
"Thank you, Father Dear!"

F
Father's Day, Father's Day,

It is almost here.

C7   F
Hugs and kisses to my dad,

  C7   F
I love you, Father Dear!

**Becky Valenick
Mesa, AZ**

Additional songs for Father's day may be adapted from the Mother's Day songs on pages 71 to 76.

FLAG DAY

Flag Day
Sung to: "Yankee Doodle"

C   G7
Sit down, children, look at me,

C   G
I'll tell you a story.

             C   F
You'll learn about our country's flag,

    G7
It's nickname is "Old Glory."

F
Stars and stripes are on our flag,

C
Red and white and blue,

           F
To show the world that we are free,

       C   G7   C
And proud to live here, too!

Sue Brown
Louisville, KY

Stars and Stripes
Sung to: "Row, Row, Row Your Boat"

C
Wave, wave, wave the flag,

As we march around.

Hold it high to show our pride,

   G   C
It must not touch the ground.

C
Wave, wave, wave the flag,

Dear red, white and blue.

Stars and stripes forever bright,

   G   C
America to you!

JoAnn C. Leist
Smithfield, NC

Our Flag
Sung to: "Twinkle, Twinkle, Little Star"

C   F   C
Stripes and stripes and little stars,

G7   C   G7   C
Oh, how beautiful you are.

          G7   C   G7
Red and white and blue, that's true,

C   G7   C   G7
Waving proud for me and you.

C   F   C
Stripes and stripes and little stars,

G7   C   G   C
Oh, how beautiful you are!

Becky Valenick
Mesa, AZ

We Honor You
Sung to: "Happy Birthday"

Oh, red, white and blue,

We honor you.

You have red and white stripes,

And fifty stars, too.

Jennifer Wagner
Camarillo, CA

See Our Flag
Sung to: "Mary Had a Little Lamb"

See our flag, it's waving high,

Waving high, waving high.

See our flag, it's waving high.

It's red and white and blue.

Bonnie Woodard
Shreveport, LA

Wave Your Flag
Sung to: "Row, Row, Row Your Boat"

Wave, wave, wave your flag,

Wave it to the sky.

It is red and white and blue,

Wave it way up high.

Sharon Smith
Doylestown, PA

I'm Proud of Our Flag
Sung to: "Hickory, Dickory, Dock"

Our flag is red, white and blue,

There are stars and stripes on it, too.

I'm proud of our flag, the United States flag,

And you can be proud of it, too!

Debra Lindahl
Libertyville, IL

Yankee Doodle Flag
Sung to: "Yankee Doodle"

C   G7
We will march to town today

    C   G
And have a celebration.

C   F
We will sing about our flag

    G7   C
To honor our great nation.

F
Yankee Doodle, keep it up,

C
Yankee Doodle dandy.

F
Our flag is such a special thing,

C   G   C
Let's all keep it handy.

   C   G7
We brought along some flags today

   C   G
To wave for our great nation.

C   F
Here's a flag for you to wave,

        G7   C
Please join our celebration.

F
Yankee Doodle, keep it up,

C
Yankee Doodle dandy.

F
Our flag is such a special thing,

C   G   C
Let's all keep it handy.

Jean Warren

Here's My Flag
Sung to: "Yankee Doodle"

C   G7
Here's my flag, red, white and blue,

    C   G
It flies so very proudly.

    C   F
I love my country very much,

    G7   C
I want to let you know it.

F
Fly the flag high and proud,

C
Freedom is our glory.

F
We should fly it every day

       C   G7   C
To show we love it truly.

Patricia Coyne
Mansfield, MA

Oh, When the Flags

Sung to: "When the Saints Go Marching In"

Oh, when the ^Cflags come marching in,

Oh, when the flags come marching ^Gin.

How we ^Clove to see our three ^Fcolors,

When the ^Cflags come marching ^Gin.^C

First comes the ^Cred, then white and blue,

First comes the red, then white and ^Gblue.

How we ^Clove to see our three ^Fcolors,

When the ^Cflags come marching ^Gin.^C

Oh, hear the ^Cbells come marching in,

Oh, hear the bells come marching ^Gin.

We ring the ^Cbells for our great ^Fnation,

For the ^Cred and white and ^Gblue.^C

Oh, hear the ^Cdrums come marching in,

Oh, hear the drums come marching ^Gin.

We beat the ^Cdrums for our great ^Fnation,

For the ^Cred and ^Gwhite and ^Cblue.

Oh, hear the ^Chorns come marching in,

Oh, hear the horns come marching ^Gin.

We toot the ^Chorns for our great ^Fnation,

For the ^Cred and ^Gwhite and ^Cblue.

Jean Warren

Old Glory

Sung to: "Oh, My Darling Clementine"

On a ^Fflag pole, in our city,

Waves a flag, a sight to ^{C7}see.

Colored red and white and ^Fblue,

It ^{C7}flies for me and ^Fyou.

^FOld Glory! Old Glory!

We will keep it waving ^{C7}free.

It's a symbol of our ^Fnation,

And it ^{C7}flies for you and ^Fme.

Nancy Nason Biddinger
Orlando, FL

Down at the Flagpole
Sung to: "Down by the Station"

F   C   F C7
Down at the flagpole early in morning,

F   C7   F
We will raise our flag to honor this great land.

       C7   F   C
We will play our bells as we march around it.

F   Am   B♭ C7 F
Ring, ring, ring, ring goes our band.

F   C   F C7
Down at the flagpole early in morning,

F   C7   F
We will raise our flag to honor this great land.

       C7   F   C
We will play our drums as we march around it.

F   Am   B♭ C7 F
Rat-a-tat, rat-a-tat goes our band.

F   C   F C7
Down at the flagpole early in morning,

F   C7   F
We will raise our flag to honor this great land.

       C7   F   C
We will play our horns as we march around it.

F   Am   B♭ C7 F
Toot, toot, toot, toot goes our band.

Jean Warren

Way up in the Sky
Sung to: "Row, Row, Row Your Boat"

C
Wave, wave, wave the flag,

Hold it very high.

Watch the colors gently wave,

G   C
Way up in the sky.

C
March, march, march around,

Hold the flag up high.

Wave, wave, wave the flag,

G   C
Way up in the sky.

Sue Brown
Louisville, KY

FOURTH OF JULY

July the Fourth Is Coming
Sung to: "Pop! Goes the Weasel"

C   G   C
July the Fourth is coming,

         G   C
And I can hardly wait.

           G   C
There'll be lots and lots of fireworks.

F   G C
Time to celebrate

          G   C
America's independence,

     G   C
A very special day.

            G   C
We'll wave our flags and watch parades.

F   G   C
Happy Birthday, U.S.A.!

Jennifer Wagner
Camarillo, CA

Independence Day
Sung to: "Mary Had a Little Lamb"

C
One, two, three, four — Fourth of July,

G7   C
Fourth of July, Fourth of July.

One, two, three, four — Fourth of July,

G7   C
Independence Day.

C
Flying flags with red, white and blue,

G7   C
Red, white and blue; red, white and blue.

Flying flags with red, white and blue,

G7   C
Independence Day.

Carla C. Skjong
Tyler, MN

Designs in the Sky
Sung to: "Frere Jacques"

C
Fourth of July, Fourth of July,

It is fun, it is fun.

A picnic in the park,

And then after dark,

C
Designs in the sky, Fourth of July.

Saundra Winnett
Lewisville, TX

The Fourth Day of July
Sung to: "Yankee Doodle"

C   G7
Picnics, parades and fireworks, too,

C   G
Exploding in the sky.

C   F
This is how we celebrate

G7   C
The Fourth Day of July.

Sue Brown
Louisville, KY

On the Fourth of July
Sung to: "London Bridge"

C
It's our country's birthday,

G7   C
Birthday, birthday.

It's our country's birthday,

G7   C
On the Fourth of July!

Becky Valenick
Mesa, AZ

Our Nation's Birthday
Sung to: "Frere Jacques"

C
July Fourth, July Fourth,

Is the date, is the date,

Of our nation's birthday,

Of our nation's birthday.

C
Celebrate! Celebrate!

Bonnie Woodard
Shreveport, LA

See the Parade
Sung to: "If You're Happy and You Know It"

Oh, ^Gsee the parade going ^Dby.

Oh, see the parade going ^Gby.

Oh, ^Cfunny clowns and marching bands,

It's ^GFourth of July!

Oh, ^Dsee the parade going ^Gby.

Oh, ^Gwatch the fireworks up in the ^Dsky.

Oh, watch the fireworks up in the ^Gsky.

^CDifferent colors in the sky,

It's ^GFourth of July!

Oh, ^Dwatch the fireworks up in the ^Gsky.

Debra Butler
Denver, CO

Sputter, Sputter, Fourth of July
Sung to: "Twinkle, Twinkle, Little Star"

^CSputter, sputter ^Fup so ^Chigh,

^{G7}We can ^Csee the ^{G7}lighted ^Csky.

^{G7}Celebrating the ^CFourth of ^{G7}July,

^CIllu^{G7}minations ^Cup so ^{G7}high.

^CSputter, sputter ^Fup so ^Chigh,

^{G7}Bang and ^Cburst — "Hurray!" ^{G7}we ^Ccry.

Susan Peters
Upland, CA

Wave a Little Flag
Sung to: "I'm a Little Teapot"

^CWave a little flag,

^FRed, white and ^Cblue.

^{G7}Our country belongs

^{G7}To ^Cme and you.

So, all together ^Fwe can ^Csay,

^F"Happy ^{G7}Independence ^CDay!"

Barbara Paxson
Warren, OH

It's the Fourth of July
Sung to: "Row, Row, Row Your Boat"

C
Eat, eat, eat the food,

It's picnic time once more.

Hot dogs, burgers and apple pie,

     G   C
Let's hope the rain won't pour!

C
Play, play, play the games,

The gang's together now.

Racing, throwing, pitching, rowing,

     G   C
Please now take a bow!

C
Bang, pop, crackle, hiss!

The fireworks light the sky.

We all are here to celebrate,

     G   C
Because it's Fourth of July!

Debra Lindahl
Libertyville, IL

On Independence Day
Sung to: "Mary Had a Little Lamb"

C
Fireworks go snap, snap, snap!

G7   C
Crack, crack, crack! Zap, zap, zap!

Fireworks make me clap, clap, clap

    G7   C
On Independence Day!

Barbara Paxson
Warren, OH

Hurrah for July Fourth!
Sung to: "The Muffin Man"

F
Oh, hurrah for July Fourth,

G7   C7
July Fourth, July Fourth.

          F
Oh, hurrah for July Fourth,

   G7   C   F
It comes just once a year.

F
Let's go to the picnic,

      G7   C7
The fireworks, the parade.

F
There's so much to do today,

          G7   C   F
To celebrate Independence Day!

Patricia Coyne
Mansfield, MA

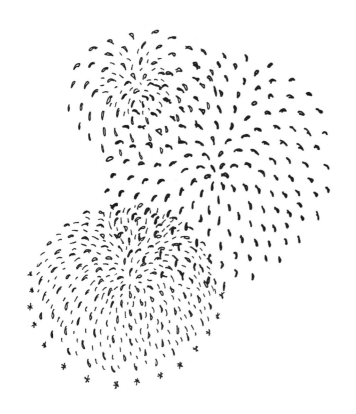

At the Fireworks Show
Sung to: "London Bridge"

C
All together here we go,

G7   C
Here we go, here we go.

All together here we go

      G7   C
To the fireworks show.

C
I like fireworks, don't you, too,

G7   C
Don't you, too; don't you, too?

I like fireworks, don't you, too?

     G7   C
At the fireworks show.

C
They make such a pretty sight,

G7   C
Pretty sight, pretty sight.

They make such a pretty sight.

G7   C
Wow! The fireworks show.

Becky Valenick
Mesa, AZ

Fireworks
Sung to: "Ten Little Indians"

C
Fireworks bursting in the night,
   (Open and close hands quickly.)

G7
Watch them make a beautiful sight.
   (Pretend to look through binoculars.)

C
They give off a sparkling light.
   (Open and close hands quickly.)

G7   C
Hurray, Fourth of July!

5-4-3-2-1 — BOOM!
   (Jump up with arms and legs extended, then open
and close hands slowly while lowering arms.)

Vicki Claybrook
Kennewick, WA

Fireworks Light the Sky
Sung to: "Row, Row, Row Your Boat"

C
Fireworks light the sky

On the Fourth of July —

To celebrate the birthday

G   C
Of the U.S.A.

Vicki Shannon
Napton, MO

TITLE INDEX

94

Totline® Books

Super Snacks
Teaching Tips
Teaching Toys
Piggyback® Songs
More Piggyback® Songs
Piggyback® Songs for Infants and Toddlers
Piggyback® Songs in Praise of God
Piggyback® Songs in Praise of Jesus
Holiday Piggyback® Songs
Animal Piggyback® Songs
Piggyback® Songs for School

1·2·3 Art
1·2·3 Games
1·2·3 Colors
1·2·3 Puppets
1·2·3 Murals
1·2·3 Books
Teeny-Tiny Folktales
Short-Short Stories
Mini-Mini Musicals
Small World Celebrations
Special Day Celebrations
Yankee Doodle Birthday Celebrations
Great Big Holiday Celebrations
"Cut & Tell" Scissor Stories for Fall
"Cut & Tell" Scissor Stories for Winter
"Cut & Tell" Scissor Stories for Spring
Seasonal Fun
Alphabet Theme-A-Saurus
Theme-A-Saurus
Theme-A-Saurus II
Toddler Theme-A-Saurus
Alphabet & Number Rhymes
Color, Shape & Season Rhymes
Object Rhymes
Animal Rhymes
Our World
"Mix & Match" Animal Patterns
"Mix & Match" Everyday Patterns
"Mix & Match" Holiday Patterns
"Mix & Match" Nature Patterns
ABC Space
ABC Farm
ABC Zoo
ABC Circus

**Available at school supply stores and parent/teacher stores
or write for our catalog.**

Warren Publishing House, Inc. • P.O. Box 2250, Dept. B • Everett, WA 98203